Copyright © 2017 by Consie Berghausen

Published and distributed by RICHER Press

Cover Design: RICHER Media USA

Illustrations: Nina Berghausen

No part of this publication may be reproduced, stored in a retrieval system, or transmitted in any form or by any means, electronic, mechanical, photocopying, recording, scanning, or otherwise, except as permitted under Section 107 or 108 of the 1976 United States Copyright Act, without prior written permission of the publisher.

Library of Congress Cataloging-in-Publications Data: 2017932542

Consie Berghausen

**A Shark! Named Jamison**

1st   edition

p.     cm.

1. Children 2. Education 3. Reference

ISBN 13: 978-0-9970831-9-4 (Paperback)

First edition, March 2017

**Printed in the United States of America**

## DEDICATION

"To my children and grandchildren and to Jamison's rescuers"

## PARENTS CORNER

Take the time to share some of these basic facts about sharks with your children. It will help them better understand Jamison's amazing adventure.

## BASIC FACTS ABOUT SHARKS

- There are more than 465 known species of sharks living in our oceans today.
- Sharks belong to a family of fish.
- Sharks have skeletons made of cartilage, a tissue more flexible and lighter than bone.
- Shark 'skin' is made up of a series of scales that act as an outer skeleton for easy movement and for saving energy in the water.
- Sharks breathe through a series of five to seven gill slits located on either side of their bodies.
- All sharks have multiple rows of teeth, and while they lose teeth on a regular basis, new teeth continue to grow in and replace the old ones.
- The upper side of a shark is generally dark to blend in with the water from above and their undersides are white or lighter colored to blend in with the lighter surface of the sea from below.

Jamison and Mom swim in the ocean,
Cruising together in rhythmic motion.
Jamison's young and follows her closely
Through dark waters with swells that look ghostly.

He is six feet long and six months old.
He's learning a lot and does what he's told.
Many questions he still asks his Mother.
He is without a sister or brother.

Summer is coming; it's time to head north.
Traveling the coastline their plan is set forth.
Mom says, "We will stop when we reach Cape Cod."
Jamison listens and gives her a nod.

Mom adds, "We'll head to a place
known as Chatham,
With shallows and shoals where the sand flattens.
Chatham Lighthouse sends forth
beams day and night.
We will have arrived when we see that light.
There are oodles of grey and harbor seals
Who play and frolic and make tasty meals.

"There are shivers of sharks who summer there,
With friends a plenty we won't have a care."
When they arrived there were sharks all around,
Some deep, some shallow, all harbor-seal bound.

But there were no other sharks of his age.
Frolicking near big sharks just made them rage.
The seals were his size but darted away
And left him alone with nothing but spray.

Cruising the surf all alone for the day
The sharks rejected his plea to come play.
And then he saw him, this cute little guy!
Yellow beak, grey wings, and two beady eyes.

Close to the water and up on the sand
Jamison thought, *I could go on the land!*
To meet his new friend, this seagull, this bird,
With Mother nearby, he said not a word.
He was used to doing what he was told
But getting older he now felt more bold.

He swam so fast that he leapt in the air,
A split second flying without a care.
Then oomph, ouch, splat, yikes, he landed on ground.
He was hurt and heavy and not water bound.

The seagull flew off, leaving Jamison stuck.
No breaths and no Mom, just out of luck.
Except that it was a lovely beach day
For swimming and picnics and catching rays.

A group of beach goers with hearts of gold
Came running to help when they are first told,
"There's a young great white shark
here in the sand.
He's in need of aid,
let's give him a hand."

With buckets of water thrown on his gills,
Jamison breathes while he's lying quite still.
Then he starts moving and the people cheer,
"Let's move him to water and gather gear."

A boat and a rope is all that it takes,
And hopefully there will be no mistakes
Handling this most dangerous creature,
Teeth being his most prominent feature.

The Harbormaster and a special team
Tie the rope to his tail and to the beam
Of their boat and tow Jamison seaward,
Watching the shark as they proceed leeward.

Jamison receives a special shark tag.
"He's the youngest to get one,"
his Mom brags.
Now free in the sea,
sharks friend him at last.
Playing alone is a thing of the past.

A real shark hero who went up on shore,
A place where no great white ventured before.
Jamison whispers and Mom gives a nod
"Let's always summer *off* shore in Cape Cod."

# The Team: Consie and Nina Berghausen

Consie splits her time between Tucson, Arizona and Chatham, Massachusetts. Her home in Chatham is on a saltwater marsh. It is her many years of watching wildlife out her back window that inspired her debut novel, *The Saltwater Marsh, a Magical Place*. She and Riverhaven books most recently teamed up to publish her next story set in Chatham, *The Cormorant and the Clam*. A teacher and former therapist, Consie now enjoys writing about nature and wildlife. She plays the piano and a mean game of tennis.

Nina is a graphic design artist in California. She enjoys working at the public library, playing tennis, and horseback riding. She also has a heart for animals.

**Website:** www.consieberghausen.com

**Facebook:** www.facebook.com/consieandninaberghausen

**Email:** 22consie@gmail.com

CPSIA information can be obtained
at www.ICGtesting.com
Printed in the USA
BVHW02s0618190618
519394BV00002B/2/P